# <u>INDEX</u>

# Once upon a time: Zarqawi

On a cold and blustery evening in December 1989, Huthaifa Azzam, the teenage son of the legendary Jordanian-Palestinian mujahideen leader Sheikh Abdullah Azzam, went to the airport in Peshawar, Pakistan, to welcome a group of young men. All were new recruits, largely from Jordan, and they had come to fight in a fratricidal civil war in neighboring Afghanistan—an outgrowth of the CIA-financed jihad of the 1980s against the Soviet occupation there.

The men were scruffy, Huthaifa mused as he greeted them, and seemed hardly in battle-ready form. Some had just been released from prison; others were professors and sheikhs. None of them would prove worth remembering— except for a relatively short, squat man named Ahmad Fadhil Nazzal al-Khalaylah. He would later rename himself Abu Musab al-Zarqawi.

Once one of the most wanted men in the world, for whose arrest the United States offered a $25 million reward, al-Zarqawi was a notoriously enigmatic figure—a man who was everywhere yet nowhere.

Huthaifa Azzam bridges both worlds. He first went into battle at the age of fifteen, fighting against the Soviets in Afghanistan with his father and Osama bin Laden (to whom his father was a spiritual mentor); three years later, on that December night at the Peshawar airport, he met al-Zarqawi for the first time. The two Azzams and bin Laden had fought against the Soviets in the early days of the jihad; al-Zarqawi would fight in the war's second phase, after the Soviets had pulled out. Both Huthaifa Azzam and al-Zarqawi would eventually leave Afghanistan to pursue two very different lives, but their paths would once again cross on the battlefields of jihad in Iraq, after the U.S. invasion of 2003.

A self-described jihadist—one who believes in struggle, or, more loosely, holy war—Azzam now lives in the Jordanian capital, Amman, where he is at work on a doctorate in classical Arabic literature, but he moves routinely between Jordan and Iraq.

Abu Musab al-Zarqawi, barely forty and barely literate, a Bedouin from the Bani Hassan tribe, was until recently almost unknown outside his native Jordan.

Then, on February 5, 2003, Secretary of State Colin Powell catapulted him onto the world stage. In his address to the United Nations making the case for war in Iraq, Powell identified al-Zarqawi—mistakenly, as it turned out—as the crucial link between al-Qaeda and Saddam Hussein's regime. Subsequently, al-Zarqawi became a leading figure in the insurgency in Iraq—and in November of last year, he also brought his jihadist revolution back home, as the architect of three lethal hotel bombings in Amman.

His notoriety grew with every atrocity he perpetrated, yet Western and Middle Eastern intelligence officials remained bedeviled by a simple question: Who was he? Was he al-Qaeda's point man in Iraq, as the Bush administration argued repeatedly? Or was he, as a retired Israeli intelligence official told not long ago, a staunch rival of bin Laden's, whose importance the United States exaggerated in order to validate a link between al-Qaeda and pre-war Iraq, and to put a non-Iraqi face on a complex insurgency?

Bin Laden and Zarqawi had little in common: bin Laden, like most of his inner circle, is a university graduate from an influential family; al-Zarqawi, like many who follow him, was from an anonymous family (even though they are members of a significant tribe) and an anonymous town—a man who was fired from a job as a video-store clerk and whose background included street gangs and, according to Jordanian intelligence officials, prison for sexual assault. He was a ruthless self-promoter who, U.S. officials claim, killed or wounded thousands of people in three years (2003-2006)—in suicide bombings, mass executions, and beheadings that have been videotaped. He developed a mythic aura of invulnerability. But he was not the terrorist mastermind that he was often claimed to be.

Zarqa is a shambolic industrial city of some 850,000 people, a sprawl of factories, open fields, and dust. Twenty-five miles northeast of Amman, it is Jordan's third-largest city, and one of its most militant. For years it has been a magnet for Islamic activists. Along with the cities of Irbid and Salt, it has sent the largest number of Jordanian volunteers to fight abroad, first in Afghanistan and now in Iraq. Al-Zarqawi was born and raised in the al-Masoum neighborhood of Zarqa's old city, which sprawls somewhat haphazardly into the al-Ruseifah Palestinian refugee camp. (*More than 60 percent of Jordan's 5.9 million inhabitants are Palestinian, as are some 80 percent of the inhabitants of old Zarqa.*)

Until his death, al-Zarqawi kept a home on a quiet lane in Zarqa. It was indistinguishable from its neighbors—a two-story white stucco building surrounded by a whitewashed wall. The house was empty,; al-Zarqawi's sisters, who still live in Zarqa, would come by to look after it.

The first of al-Zarqawi's two wives had lived in the house until recently. She was his cousin, whom he had married when he was twenty-two. They had four children, two boys and two girls. But not long before my visit, al-Zarqawi had sent an unknown man to drive them across the border to be with him in Iraq. His second wife, a Jordanian-Palestinian whom he had married in Afghanistan, and with whom he has a son, was reported to be with him in Iraq as well. Al-Zarqawi's mother, Omm Sayel, whom he adored—and who had traveled to Peshawar with him when he joined the jihad—died of leukemia in 2004; although he was the most wanted man in Jordan at the time of her death, al-Zarqawi returned to Zarqa in disguise to attend her funeral.

## Afganistan

Al-Zarqawi was based initially in the border town of Khost, which, after both the Americans and the Soviets had left Afghanistan, was the site of intense and heavily contested battles between the mujahideen and the pro-Soviet Najibullah regime. At the beginning, al-Zarqawi had not been a fighter but had tried his hand at being a journalist. He had worked as a reporter for a small jihadist magazine, *Al-Bonian al Marsous*.

"*He was an ordinary guy, an ordinary fighter, and didn't really distinguish himself,*" Huthaifa Azzam said of al-Zarqawi's first time in Afghanistan. "*He was a quiet guy who didn't talk much. But he was brave. Zarqawi doesn't know the meaning of fear. He's been wounded five or six times in Afghanistan and Iraq. He seems to intentionally place himself in the middle of the most dangerous situations. He fought in the battles of Khost and Kardez and, in April 1992, witnessed the liberation of Kabul by the mujahideen. A lot of Arabs were great commanders during those years. Zarqawi was not. He also wasn't very religious during that time. In fact, he'd only 'returned' to Islam three months before coming to Afghanistan. It was the Tablighi Jamaat* [a proselytizing missionary group spread across the Muslim world] *who convinced him—he had thirty-seven criminal cases against him by then—that it was time to cleanse himself.*"

His second time in Afghanistan was far more important than the first. But the first was significant in two ways. Zarqawi was young and impressionable; he'd never been out of Jordan before, and now, for the first time, he was interacting with doctrinaire Islamists from across the Muslim world, most of them brought to Afghanistan by the CIA. It was also his first exposure to al-Qaeda. He didn't meet bin Laden, of course, but he trained in one of his and Abdullah Azzam's camps: the Sada camp near the Afghan border inside Pakistan. He trained under Abu Hafs al-Masri." (*The reference was to the nom de guerre of Mohammed Atef, an Egyptian who was bin Laden's military chief and, until he was killed in an American air strike in Afghanistan in November 2001, the No. 3 official in al-Qaeda.*)

Abu Muntassir Bilah Muhammad is another jihadist who spent time fighting in Afghanistan and who would later become one of the co-founders of al-Zarqawi's first militant Islamist group. "*Zarqawi arrived in Afghanistan as a zero, a man with no career, just floundering about. He trained and fought and he came back to Jordan with ambitions and dreams: to carry the ideology of jihad. His first ambition was to reform Jordan, to set up an Islamist state. And there was a cachet involved in fighting in the jihad. Zarqawi returned to Jordan with newfound respect. It's not so much what Zarqawi did in the jihad—it's what the jihad did for him.*"

With an eye to the future, al-Zarqawi also used the jihad years to begin the process of cultivating friendships that would eventually lead to the formation of an international support network for his activities. Particularly when he was in Khost, his primary friendships were with the Saudi fighters and others from the Gulf. Some of them were millionaires. There were even a couple of billionaires.

But perhaps as important as anything else, it was in Afghanistan that al-Zarqawi was introduced to Sheikh Abu Muhammad al-Maqdisi (*whose real name is Isam Muhammad Tahir al-Barqawi*), a revered and militant Salafist cleric who had moved to Zarqa following the mass expulsion of Palestinians from Kuwait in the aftermath of the Gulf War. The Salafiya movement originated in Egypt, at the end of the nineteenth century, as a modernist Sunni reform movement, the aim of which was to let the Muslim world rise to the challenges posed by Western science and political thought. But since the 1920s, it has evolved into a severely puritanical school of absolutist thought that is markedly anti-Western and based on a literal interpretation of the Koran.

Today's most radical Salafists regard any departure from their own rigid principles of Islam to be heretical; their particular hatred of Shiites—who broke with the Sunnis in 632 A.D. over the question of succession to the Prophet Muhammad, and who now constitute the majority in Iran and Iraq—is visceral. Over the years, al-Maqdisi embraced the most extreme school of Salafism, closely akin to the puritanical Wahhabism of Saudi Arabia, and in the early 1980s he published *The Creed of Abraham*, the single most important source of teachings for Salafist movements around the world.

Al-Zarqawi and al-Maqdisi left Afghanistan in 1993 and returned to Jordan. They found it much changed. In their absence the Jordanians and the Israelis had begun negotiations that would lead to the signing of a peace treaty in 1994; the Palestinians had signed the Oslo Accords of 1993; and the Iraqis had lost the Gulf War. Unemployment was up sharply, the result of a privatization drive agreed to with the International Monetary Fund, and Jordanians were frustrated and angry. The Muslim Brotherhood—the kingdom's only viable opposition political force, which had agreed to support King Hussein in exchange for being allowed to participate in public and parliamentary life—appeared unable to cope with the rising disaffection. Small underground Islamist groups had therefore begun to appear, composed largely of men who had fought in the Afghan jihad, and who were guided by the increasingly loud voices of militant clerics who felt the Muslim Brotherhood had been co-opted by the state.

After the two men returned home, al-Maqdisi toured the kingdom, preaching and recruiting, and al-Zarqawi sought out Abu Muntassir, who had already acquired a standing among Islamic militants in Jordan. Despite their enthusiasm, al-Zarqawi, al-Maqdisi, and Abu Muntassir did not appear to be natural revolutionaries. Their first operation was in Zarqa, in 1993, when al-Zarqawi dispatched one of their men to a local cinema with orders to blow it up because it was showing pornographic films. But the hapless would-be bomber apparently got so distracted by what was happening on the screen that he forgot about his bomb. It exploded and blew off his legs.

In another botched operation, al-Maqdisi (according to court testimony that he denied) gave al-Zarqawi seven grenades he had smuggled into Jordan, and al-Zarqawi hid them in the cellar of his family's home. Al-Maqdisi was already under surveillance by Jordan's intelligence service by that time, because of his growing popularity. The grenades were quickly discovered, and the two men, along with a number of their followers, found themselves for the first time before a state security court. Al-Zarqawi told the court that he had found the grenades while walking down the street. The judges were not amused. They convicted him and al-Maqdisi of possessing illegal weapons and belonging to a banned organization. In 1994, al-Zarqawi was sentenced to fifteen years in prison. He would flourish there.

Al-Zarqawi embraced prison life in the extreme—as he appears to have embraced everything. According to fellow inmates of his, his primary obsessions were recruiting other prisoners to his cause, building his body, and, under the tutelage of al-Maqdisi, memorizing the 6,236 verses of the Koran. He was stern, tough, and unrelenting on anything that he considered to be an infraction of his rules, yet he was often seen in the prison courtyard crying as he read the Koran.

He was fastidious about his appearance in prison—his beard and moustache were always cosmetically groomed—and he wore only Afghan dress: the *shalwar kameez* and a rolled-brim, woolen Pashtun cap. Islamists flocked to him. He attracted recruits; some joined him out of fascination, others out of curiosity, and still others out of fear. In a short time, he had organized prison life at Swaqa like a gang leader.

There were also confrontations and altercations with prison officials and guards. Whether al-Zarqawi was ever tortured is a matter of dispute: some of his followers say he was; Jordanian government officials, perhaps predictably, say he was not.

Al-Zarqawi controlled not only his followers but also the ward's television sets. No one could really *watch* them, however, since he had covered them with black cloth to prevent the display of female forms. All the inmates could do was listen—and only to the evening news at eight o'clock.

Al-Zarqawi and al-Maqdisi's Bayat al-Imam continued to grow, both inside prison and in Zarqa, Irbid, and Salt. Al-Zarqawi used his Bedouin credentials to good effect, as his own profile began to ascend. His Bani Hassan tribe is one of the Middle East's most prominent, and its tribal lands spill across the borders dividing Jordan, Syria, and Iraq. In Jordan, many of its members hold high-level positions in the government, the army, and the intelligence service. As a result, many of the prisoners, and many of Swaqa's guards, deferred to al-Zarqawi. Al-Maqdisi, a Palestinian, was also accorded special treatment, but largely as a result of his links to al-Zarqawi and the Bani Hassan. Between mentor and pupil, the roles had subtly begun to shift inside the prison walls.

As al-Zarqawi recruited, al-Maqdisi preached, and using the Internet, they broadcast their message of jihad across three continents. Sheikh Abu Qatada, a Palestinian cleric who is one of Salafism's leading ideologues, was also one of al-Maqdisi's closest friends. The two men had been together in Kuwait, then in Zarqa, then Afghanistan. Abu Qatada, after leaving Afghanistan, had moved to London (where he is currently under arrest, awaiting possible deportation to Jordan). Now al-Maqdisi's religious tracts were smuggled out of Swaqa by prisoners' wives and mothers, with help from sympathetic prison guards, and they were sent on to Abu Qatada, who posted them on the Web sites of Salafists and jihadists throughout Europe, the Middle East, and the Persian Gulf.

Al-Zarqawi's own religious views became increasingly severe, as did his intolerance of anyone he believed to be an infidel. Al-Maqdisi sometimes angrily disagreed with him. It was the first portent of what lay ahead. Al-Zarqawi began to eclipse his mentor in prison, and would continue to do so over the coming years, but their final, and public, break did not occur until November 2005, when, on Al-Jazeera, al-Maqdisi criticized his former protégé for the hotel bombings in Amman. Nevertheless, despite their prison disagreements, al-Maqdisi, from time to time, permitted al-Zarqawi to draft his own religious tracts. Abu Muntassir who would also later break with al-Zarqawi was his editor.

In May of the following year (1999), Jordan's King Abdullah II—newly enthroned after the death of his father, King Hussein—declared a general amnesty, and al-Zarqawi was released from Swaqa. He had made effective use of his time there. As he had done nearly a decade before—when he befriended wealthy Saudi jihadists in Khost—he had expanded his reach and his appeal during his prison years. Among the fellow inmates he had converted to Salafism and brought into the Bayat al-Imam were a substantial number of prisoners from Iraq.

After returning for a few months to Zarqa, al-Zarqawi left again and traveled to Pakistan. He may or may not have known that Jordan was about to declare him a suspect in a series of foiled terrorist attacks intended for New Year's Eve of 1999. The plan, which became known as the "Millennium Plot," involved the bombing of Christian landmarks and other tourist sites, along with the Radisson Hotel in Amman. Had it succeeded, it would have been al-Zarqawi's first involvement in a major terrorist attack.

Whatever the case, al-Zarqawi planned ahead before he left for Pakistan. He arrived bearing a letter of introduction from Abu Kutaiba al-Urduni, one of Jordan's most significant leaders during the jihad in Afghanistan. Al-Urduni had been a key deputy to—and the chief recruiter inside Jordan for—Sheikh Abdullah Azzam, Huthaifa Azzam's father. Having worked for years in Peshawar as the leader of the Service Office, or the Maktab al-Khidmat, the sheikh had become *the* pivotal figure in the Pan-Islamic recruitment of volunteers for the jihad.) Al-Urduni's letter was the first endorsement that al-Zarqawi had received from such a senior figure—and the letter was addressed to Osama bin Laden.

In December 1999, al-Zarqawi crossed the border into Afghanistan, and later that month he and bin Laden met at the Government Guest House in the southern city of Kandahar, the de facto capital of the ruling Taliban. According to several different accounts of the meeting, bin Laden distrusted and disliked al-Zarqawi immediately. He suspected that the group of Jordanian prisoners with whom al-Zarqawi had been granted amnesty earlier in the year had been infiltrated by Jordanian intelligence.

Something similar had occurred not long before with a Jordanian jihadist cell that had come to Afghanistan. Bin Laden also disliked al-Zarqawi's swagger and the green tattoos on his left hand, which he reportedly considered un-Islamic. Al-Zarqawi came across to bin Laden as aggressively ambitious, abrasive, and overbearing. His hatred of Shiites also seemed to bin Laden to be potentially divisive—which, of course, it was. Bin Laden's mother, to whom he remains close, is a Shiite, from the Alawites of Syria.

Al-Zarqawi would not recant, even in the presence of the legendary head of al-Qaeda. "Shiites should be executed," he reportedly declared. He also took exception to bin Laden's providing Arab fighters to the Taliban, the fundamentalist student militia that, although now in power, was still battling the Northern Alliance, which controlled some 10 percent of Afghanistan. Muslim killing Muslim was un-Islamic, al-Zarqawi is reported to have said. Unaccustomed to such direct criticism, the leader of al-Qaeda was aghast.

A former Egyptian army colonel who had trained in special operations, al-Adel was then al-Qaeda's chief of security and a prominent voice in an emerging debate gripping the militant Islamist world. Who should the primary target be—the "near enemy" (the Muslim world's "un-Islamic" regimes) or the "far enemy" (primarily Israel and the United States)? Al-Zarqawi was a near-enemy advocate, and although his obsession remained the overthrow of the Jordanian monarchy, he had expanded his horizons slightly during his prison years and had now begun to focus on the area known as al-Sham, or the Levant, which includes Jordan, Syria, Lebanon, and historic Palestine.

As an Egyptian who had attempted to overthrow his own country's army-backed regime, al-Adel saw merit in al-Zarqawi's views. Thus, after a good deal of debate within al-Qaeda, it was agreed that al-Zarqawi would be given $5,000 or so in "seed money" to set up his own training camp outside the western Afghan city of Herat, near the Iranian border. It was about as far away as he could be from bin Laden. Saif al-Adel was designated the middleman.

In early 2000, with a dozen or so followers who had arrived from Peshawar and Amman, al-Zarqawi set out for the western desert encircling Herat. His goal: to build an army that he could export to anywhere in the world. Al-Adel paid monthly visits to al-Zarqawi's training camp; later, on his Web site, he would write that he was amazed at what he saw there. The number of al-Zarqawi's fighters multiplied from dozens to hundreds during the following year, and by the time the forces evacuated their camp, prior to the U.S. air strikes of October 2001, the fighters and their families numbered some 2,000 to 3,000. According to al-Adel, the wives of al-Zarqawi's followers served lavish Levantine cuisine in the camp.

It was in Herat that al-Zarqawi formed the militant organization Jund al-Sham, or Soldiers of the Levant. His key operational lieutenants were mainly Syrians—most of whom had fought in the Afghan jihad, and many of whom belonged to their country's banned Muslim Brotherhood. The Brotherhood's exiled leadership, which is largely based in Europe, was immensely important in recruiting for the Herat camp, although whether it also supplied funds remains under debate. What is clear, however, is that al-Zarqawi's closest aide, a Syrian from the city of Hama named Sulayman Khalid Darwish—or Abu al-Ghadiyah—was considered to be, one of al-Zarqawi's most likely successors.

For Zarqawi, it was the turning point. Herat was the beginning of what he is now. He had command responsibilities for the first time; he had a battle plan. And even though he and bin Laden never got on, he was important to them. Herat was the only training camp in Afghanistan that was actively recruiting volunteers specifically from the Sham. In Herat, he called himself the 'Emir of Sham'!"

At least five times, in 2000 and 2001, bin Laden called al-Zarqawi to come to Kandahar and pay *bayat*—take an oath of allegiance—to him. Each time, al-Zarqawi refused. Under no circumstances did he want to become involved in the battle between the Northern Alliance and the Taliban. He also did not believe that either bin Laden or the Taliban was serious enough about jihad.

When the United States launched its air war inside Afghanistan, on October 7, 2001, al-Zarqawi joined forces with al-Qaeda and the Taliban for the first time. He and his Jund al-Sham fought in and around Herat and Kandahar. Al-Zarqawi was wounded in an American air strike—not in the leg, as U.S. officials claimed for two years, but in the chest, when the ceiling of the building in which he was operating collapsed on him. Neither did he join Osama bin Laden in the eastern mountains of Tora Bora, as U.S. officials have also said. Bin Laden took only his most trusted fighters to Tora Bora, and al-Zarqawi was not one of them.

In December 2001, accompanied by some 300 fighters from Jund al-Sham, al-Zarqawi left Afghanistan once again, and entered Iran.

During the next fourteen months, al-Zarqawi based himself primarily in Iran and in the autonomous area of Kurdistan, in northern Iraq, traveling from time to time to Syria and to the Ayn al-Hilwah Palestinian refugee camp in the south of Lebanon—a camp that became his main recruiting ground. More often, however, al-Zarqawi traveled to the Sunni Triangle of Iraq. He expanded his network, recruited and trained new fighters, and set up bases, safe houses, and military training camps. In Iran, he was reunited with Saif al-Adel—who encouraged him to go to Iraq and provided contacts there—and for a time, al-Zarqawi stayed at a farm belonging to the fiercely anti-American Afghan jihad leader Gulbaddin Hekmatyar. In Kurdistan he lived and worked with the separatist militant Islamist group Ansar al-Islam, ironically in an area protected as part of the "no-fly" zone imposed on Saddam Hussein by Washington.

One can only imagine how astonished al-Zarqawi must have been when Colin Powell named him as the crucial link between al-Qaeda and Saddam Hussein's regime. He was not even officially a part of al-Qaeda, and ever since he had left Afghanistan, his links had been not to Iraq but to Iran.

In the beginning the Iranians gave him automatic weapons, uniforms, military equipment, when he was with the army of Ansar al-Islam. Now they essentially just turn a blind eye to his activities, and to those of al-Qaeda generally. The

Iranians see Iraq as a fight against the Americans, and overall, they'll get rid of Zarqawi and all of his people once the Americans are out.

In the summer of 2003, three months after the American invasion, al-Zarqawi moved to the Sunni areas of Iraq. He became infamous almost at once. On August 7, he allegedly carried out a car-bomb attack at the Jordanian embassy in Baghdad. Twelve days later, he was linked to the bombing of the United Nations headquarters, in which twenty-two people died. And on August 29, in what was then the deadliest attack of the war, he engineered the killing of over a hundred people, including a revered cleric, the Ayatollah Muhammad Baqr al-Hakim, in a car bombing outside Shia Islam's holy shrine in Najaf. The suicide bomber in that attack was Yassin Jarad, from Zarqa. He was al-Zarqawi's father-in-law.

Even then—and even more so now—Zarqawi was not the main force in the insurgency. To establish himself, he carried out the Muhammad Hakim operation, and the attack against the UN. Both of them gained a lot of support for him—with the tribes, with Saddam's army and other remnants of his regime. They made Zarqawi the *symbol* of the resistance in Iraq, but not the leader. And he never has been."

The Americans have been patently stupid in all of this. They've blown Zarqawi so out of proportion that, of course, his prestige has grown. And as a result, sleeper cells from all over Europe are coming to join him now.

Of course, no one did more to cultivate that image than al-Zarqawi himself. He committed some of the deadliest attacks in Iraq, though they still represent only some 10 percent of the country's total number of attacks. In May 2004, he inaugurated his notorious wave of hostage beheadings; he also specialized in suicide and truck bombings of Shiite shrines and mosques, largely in Shiite neighborhoods. His primary aim was to provoke a civil war. "*If we succeed in dragging [the Shia] into a sectarian war,*" he purportedly wrote in a letter intercepted by U.S. forces and released in February 2004, "*this will awaken the sleepy Sunnis who are fearful of destruction and death at the hands of the Shia.*"

Al-Zarqawi courted chaos so that Iraq would provide him another failed state to operate in after the overthrow of the Taliban in Afghanistan. He became best known for his videotaped beheadings. One after the other they appeared on jihadist Web sites, always the same. In the background was the trademark black banner of al-Zarqawi's newest group: al-Tawhid wa al-Jihad, or Monotheism and Jihad. In the foreground, a blindfolded hostage, kneeling and pleading for his life, was dressed in an orange jumpsuit resembling those worn by the detainees at Guantánamo Bay.

Al-Zarqawi's first victim was a Pennsylvania engineer named Nicholas Berg. In the video, five hooded men, dressed in black, stand behind Berg. After a recitation, one of the men pulls a long knife from his shirt, steps forward, and slices off Berg's head. The U.S. military quickly announced that the executioner was al-Zarqawi himself, and although no one doubts that he planned the operation, questions soon arose: the figure seems taller than al-Zarqawi, and he uses his right hand to wield the knife. Al-Zarqawi was said to be left-handed.

Regardless of his growing notoriety in Iraq, al-Zarqawi never lost sight of his ultimate goal: the overthrow of the Jordanian monarchy. His efforts to foment unrest in Jordan included the 2002 assassination of the U.S. diplomat Lawrence Foley, and, on a far larger scale, a disrupted plot in 2004 to bomb the headquarters of the Jordanian intelligence services—a scheme that, according to Jordanian officials, would have entailed the use of trucks packed with enough chemicals and explosives to kill some 80,000 people. Once it was uncovered, al-Zarqawi immediately accepted responsibility for the plot, although he denied that chemical weapons would have been involved.

Later that year, in October 2004, after resisting for nearly five years, al-Zarqawi finally paid *bayat* to Osama bin Laden—but only after eight months of often stormy negotiations. After doing so he proclaimed himself to be the "Emir of al-Qaeda's Operations in the Land of Mesopotamia," a title that subordinated him to bin Laden but at the same time placed him firmly on the global stage.

One explanation for this coming together of these two former antagonists was simple: al-Zarqawi profited from the al-Qaeda franchise, and bin Laden needed a presence in Iraq. Another explanation is more complex: bin Laden laid claim to al-Zarqawi in the hopes of forestalling his emergence as the single most important terrorist figure in the world, and al-Zarqawi accepted bin Laden's endorsement to augment his credibility and to strengthen his grip on the Iraqi tribes. Both explanations are true. It was a pragmatic alliance, but tenuous from the start.

The attacks, which represented an expansion of al- Zarqawi's sophistication and reach, also showed his growing independence from the al-Qaeda chief. They came only thirteen months after he had sworn *bayat*. The alliance had already begun to fray.

The signs were visible as early as the summer of 2005. In a letter purportedly sent to al-Zarqawi in July from Ayman al-Zawahiri, the Egyptian surgeon who is bin Laden's designated heir, al-Zarqawi was chided about his tactics in Iraq. And although some experts have cast doubt on the letter's authenticity (it was released by the office of the U.S. Director of National Intelligence), few would dispute its message: namely, that al-Zarqawi's hostage beheadings, his mass slaughter of Shiites, and his assaults on their mosques were all having a negative effect on Muslim opinion—both of him and, by extension, of al-Qaeda—around the world. In one admonition, al-Zawahiri allegedly advised al-Zarqawi that a captive can be killed as easily by a bullet as by a knife.

Then, in early April, Huthaifa Azzam announced that the "Iraqi resistance's high command" had stripped al-Zarqawi of his political role and relegated him to military operations. It was the second time that al-Zarqawi's profile had seemingly been lowered—or that he had lowered it—this year. The first had come in January, when it was announced that al-Qaeda in Iraq had joined five other Sunni insurgent groups to form a coalition called the Mujahideen Shura Council. By early May, U.S. counterterrorism analysts were still puzzling over what the two events meant and what changes they could portend.

As they debated, al-Zarqawi sprang to life again, in a video posted on the Internet on April 24. It was the first time he had appeared in a jihadist videotape, and the first time he had shown his face. Dressed in black fatigues and a black cap, he had ammunition pouches strapped across his chest. He appeared fit, if overweight, as he posed in the desert firing an automatic weapon and as he sat with a group of masked aides, apparently plotting strategy. It seemed an extremely risky thing for him to do, and yet it also appeared to be very deliberate. It was a useful tool for recruitment, intending to show al-Zarqawi as both a flamboyant fighter and a pensive strategist. More important than anything else, however, it was meant to show the world that Abu Musab al-Zarqawi—the brash young man who had come of age in the rough-and-tumble of Zarqa—remained relevant.

# Al Maqdisi

It is news to few observers that thousands, even millions, of young Muslims are influenced—to some extent—by jihadi literature circulating on various Islamist websites and discussion forums. The mujahideen's use of the internet for communication, indoctrination, recruitment and public relations has been well demonstrated. Through this medium, a field of preachers and ideologues compete for the vast audience of young Muslims, attempting to sway their opinion and bring them to the "correct" practice and understanding of Islam. Those backing the global jihadi movement have succeeded in capturing this audience—perhaps more so than other contenders—and have gained a wide following of careful but loyal readers.

The literature is critical because it provides deeper motivation to the believer, who seeks ideological backing before taking action. A group of Muslim scholars—**Abu Muhammad al-Maqdisi, Abu Basir al-Tartusi, Abu Qatada al-Filistini, 'Abd al-Qadir bin 'Abd al-'Aziz** and a few other Saudi clerics—are the primary Salafi opinion-makers guiding the jihadi movement. These scholars are relied upon for their credibility since they have either been imprisoned or exiled by their home countries. They are also perceived as being true to Islam and putting the interests of Muslims before themselves, making them sincere, legitimate and incorruptible. For the mujahideen, they are portrayed as scholarly authorities and the source for doctrinal legitimacy.

Surprisingly, al-Qaeda leaders Osama bin Laden and Ayman al-Zawahiri are not highly cited in jihadi literature. They are not considered authorities in Islamic law or looked to as the ideological force behind the jihadi movement. Indeed, in the world of Salafi-Jihadi ideology, they are relatively minor players. One possible reason for this is that the two are figureheads, pioneers in carrying out successful attacks against one of the enemies of Muslims. This suggests that there is a role for charismatic leaders to bring Muslims to jihad, as soldiers to the battlefield, but there is a separate role for these Salafi scholars in setting the broader goals for the movement, the limits and terms of engagement and selecting valid and legal targets. They are, in essence, creating the Islamic legal framework for this struggle so that the basis upon which it is waged will be sound. It is then left to strategists and mujahid leaders to conduct successful campaigns within this framework.

There is no single governing body for determining Islamic law in the Muslim world. Movements tend to center around persuasive and influential scholars that can grant them legitimacy in the eyes of other Muslims. This has been the case for the Salafi movement, including militant Salafis who form the global jihadi movement. Although the mujahideen are not held accountable to their constituency, they understand the need for their fellow Muslims to support their actions, provide them with funding and safe haven and ultimately be able to mobilize them when needed. Accordingly, the advice and writings of Salafi scholars carry much weight with the mujahideen and Muslim readers—regardless of their affiliation.

For the most influential scholars of the Salafi movement, such as Abu Muhammad al-Maqdisi, Abu Qatada and Abu Basir, the end goal is never jihad itself. The objective is to bring Muslims to a Salafi reading of Islam and then to deliver salvation to the global Muslim community. As such, the primary element of the literature is the meaning and implementation of the Sharia. The scholars first bring their interpretation of Islamic law on various political and social issues and present their advice on the appropriate action. The common ground among the scholars behind the jihadi movement is their rejection of Muslims living under apostate laws and political systems governing outside what God has decreed. The required response—for all, but to differing degrees and with differing tactics—is resistance.

This drive to instill Islamic law into Muslim society, and ultimately recreate that society under their interpretation of the law, often translates into an endorsement for violent jihad as practiced by bin Laden and others. While there are many Muslim scholars who call for these sources of law to be the primary factors in how Muslims live, the important distinction lies in how one should confront political systems that rule by law other than Sharia. The debate over law and society is critical in jihadi literature. It establishes the framework through which young Muslims should struggle; for these scholars, it is clear their aim is not jihad, but the creation of such a society through jihad, an obligatory struggle for the believer.

## Biography

Asim Tahir al-Barqawi, better known as Abu Muhammad al-Maqdisi, is one of the most prolific contemporary jihadi ideologues and a classically trained scholar. He was born in Nablus in 1959, but has been imprisoned intermittently since the 1990s by the Jordanian authorities for his criticism of the government and calls for jihad. Al-Maqdisi is regarded as one of the highest living authorities in Islam for Salafis, jihadis and other conservative Sunni Muslims who share elements of his program. His imprisonment, however, seems to have had little effect on his scholarly output. He was the most frequently cited living Salafi scholar, indicating the wide range of jihadis (*from strategists to mujahideen to fellow scholars*) that cite his writings.

Al-Maqdisi is well traveled; he moved to Kuwait as a child and later undertook studies in the University of Mosul in Iraq. After that al-Maqdisi traveled through Saudi Arabia, Pakistan and Afghanistan, where he met various jihadi groups and wrote some of his most famous books, such as *Millat 'Ibrahim wa da'awet al-anbiya wa'l murseleen* (The Creed of Abraham and the Preaching of the Prophets and the Deliverers) and *Al-kawashif al-jaliyya fi kufr al-dawla al-Sa'udiyya* (The Shameful Actions Manifest in the Saudi State's Disbelief).

In 1992 al-Maqdisi returned to Jordan and started to preach his ideology, which quickly spread among some youngsters. The shaykh criticized Jordanian officials, denouncing their rule as illegitimate and opposed to the Shari`a. A combination of direct rhetoric and well-circulated stories of how he confronted the judges and his interrogators by calling them tyrants and disbelievers, soon established al-Maqdisi as a charismatic ideologue and leader of Salafi-Jiahdism.

Al-Maqdisi's texts are frequently aimed at the youth in Jordanian prisons and similar Muslims around the world that are encouraged to hold steadfast to the path of jihad in accordance with the principles of Islamic law detailed in his texts. To be sure, the legal arguments are lost on many of his students who lack formal Islamic legal training, but he provides contemporary examples to buttress his points.

Many of his texts are in response to criticisms of jihad by other Salafi clerics, typically from the Gulf states or Saudi Arabia. Other writings include the education of the next generation of leaders, numerous issues relating to resistance to tyrannical regimes and the need to uphold the Sharia and one of his most-widely read works, the Creed of Abraham, on monotheistic faiths (*which is highly critical of contemporary Christians and Jews*).

Through his writings, al-Maqdisi sets out the "correct" agenda for the various mujahideen groups to follow, what their intentions and objectives should be as they enter jihad, what preparation is required and what they should avoid (*such as hasty actions that make the mujahideen look inept, inexperienced, or indifferent to killing innocent Muslims*). There are more nuanced discussions of espionage, defining apostasy, takfir (*labeling another Muslim an unbeliever*), different examples of interaction with tyrannical rule and explanations of when resistance is obligatory for the believer. Yet, in the end, a clear direction is set out for the mujahideen and those who support their cause on how best to proceed.

Al-Maqdisi's calls for unity are respected because of the scholarly weight behind his name and reputation. This also exposes one of the movement's weaknesses, and the shortcomings of governments confronting jihadi ideologues: a blow to his standing or a publicly lost debate would likely do much more to damage the unity of the jihadi movement than would his imprisonment.

On March 12, 2008 Abu Muhammad al-Maqdisi—born Isam Muhammad Tahir al-Barqawi in 1959—was released from a Jordanian prison after almost three years imprisonment without trial. Maqdisi has long played a pivotal role in defining jihadist ideology. After taking part in the Afghan jihad of the 1980s, he refined the ideology of declaring takfir against other Muslims—i.e. defining them as apostates and thus deserving of death—leading to the creation of jihadist groups in Jordan and 1995 attacks in Saudi Arabia—whose government he had denounced as un-Islamic as early as 1989. Between 1995 and 1999, Maqdisi was imprisoned in Jordan, during which time he expanded his ideas and built new radical networks with the help of his right-hand man, Abu Musab al-Zarqawi. From 1999, Maqdisi has spent most of his time in Jordanian prisons, reemerging briefly in 2005 before being re-imprisoned for giving an interview to al-Jazeera television in which he criticized Zarqawi's attacks on civilians while reiterating his support for a broader jihad against the West and "un-Islamic" governments. Despite his long prison terms, however, Maqdisi has written and distributed several accessible books addressing key issues such as democracy, takfir and jihadist tactics, giving him an almost unmatched influence over the evolution of jihadist theory.

## *Maqdisi's Influence*

Maqdisi's latest release from prison—apparently on grounds of ill-health—was reported extensively on radical Islamic websites. Significantly, even Islamic extremists outside the Arab world reacted euphorically to the news of his release. For example, a senior member of *the islamicawakening.com* forum, a prominent English-language Salafi website, responded to news of his release by writing: "AllahuAkbar! AllahuAkbar! Nothing describes the happiness of the mu'mineen [faithful] all around the world this day. AllahuAkbar! Our beloved Shaykh is released!" Similarly, on islambase.co.uk, the online home of many British extremists, one member described his release as "the best news in ages." Their attitude suggests that despite the death of Zarqawi and his own long imprisonment, Maqdisi's teachings—a mixture of bigotry and pragmatism—are still seen as relevant. Indeed, Maqdisi's correct predictions in 2004 and 2005 that Zarqawi's attacks on Muslim civilians would undermine support for al-Qaeda both in Iraq and abroad may have further boosted his standing among Islamic extremists worldwide. In light of Maqdisi's influence and popularity it is worth examining his key ideas in detail.

## Maqdisi on Takfir

Like many jihadis, Maqdisi's ideology depends on declaring takfir against his Muslim rivals in order to permit violence against them. However, he repeatedly says that declaring takfir should not be undertaken lightly; in his 1997 book This Is Our Aqeedah (creed), he frequently quotes Qadi Iyad, a 12th century judge from Grenada, as saying: "Declaring the blood of those who pray, who are upon tawhid [belief in the unity of God], to be permissible is a serious danger".

Maqdisi adds that takfir should only be pronounced against those who have abandoned tawhid. He says a Muslim abandons tawhid, and hence Islam, if their actions show allegiance to un-Islamic entities by aiding them or participating in their legislation. In other words, he says only those who actively support non-Islamic governments or oppose jihadis should be targeted. Unlike many al-Qaeda members, Maqdisi repeatedly warns on both moral and strategic grounds against pronouncing takfir—and hence carrying out attacks— against ordinary Muslims, saying that in the absence of an Islamic state, it is understandable that many Muslims are unable to perfectly practice Islam.

In his July 2004 book, *An Appraisal of the Fruits of Jihad* (Waqafat me'a themerat al-jihad), he writes contemptuously of jihadis who "*start bombing cinemas or make plans to blow up recreation grounds, sports clubs and other such places frequented by sinful Muslims.*" Similarly, in *This is Our Aqeedah*, he criticizes extremists who kill for small infractions of Islamic principles: "*The shaving of the beard and imitation of the kuffar (infidel) and other forms of disobedience like it is a general affliction that is spread far and wide. It is not suitable by itself for evidence of takfir.*"

## On Democracy

A large proportion of Maqdisi's writings are devoted to the discussion of democracy, which he regards as one of the main threats to Islam. Maqdisi does not object to democracy as a form of representative government, however, but because legislators deliberately create man-made laws to replace or supplement the sharia (Islamic law).

Maqdisi's arguments stem from his belief that a Muslim's faith is not complete unless he lives under sharia law. As he wrote in his early 1990s book, *Democracy is a Religion* (Al-Deemoqratiyya Deen): "*Obedience in legislation is also an act of worship*". Maqdisi consequently argued that anyone seeking to create legislation to replace the sharia is effectively seeking to take the place of God. From this, he concludes that "*anyone who seeks to implement legislation created by someone other than Allah, is in fact a polytheist.*" Yet his dislike for democracy is not absolute; he accepts that consultation (shura) between a Muslim ruler and his subjects is a valid Islamic principle—but says that this principle has been hijacked by secularists to legitimize the legislative aspect of democracies. Unlike many al-Qaeda fighters, however, Maqdisi says that the illegitimacy of legislative elections does not necessarily permit attacks against anyone who votes, since some people vote only "*to choose representatives for worldly living*" rather than to subvert the sharia.

## On Jihadi Tactics

Maqdisi believes that violent jihad against non-Muslims is a core part of Islam which can be carried out by individuals at any time or place. In an interview with al-Nida magazine in 1999, he described jihad as an "*act of worship that is permissible any time*". He also says that jihad is not dependent on living in an Islamist state or having a Caliph, nor is it restricted to battlefields or places of open conflict. Despite this, however, Maqdisi criticizes would-be jihadis whose enthusiasm for glory blinds them to political and religious realities. In An Appraisal of the Fruits of Jihad, he mocks the "*youths moved by their zeal.*" He continues:

"*[They] have studied neither the sharia nor reality. They have newly begun practicing the religion and have not yet rid themselves of the arrogance, pride, and tribalism of their pre-Islamic days, such that some of them even consider it shameful, cowardly, and disgraceful to be secret and discrete. Others proclaim that they are carrying automatic weapons or bombs that they roam about with in their cars here and there, showing them to this person and that person; they think it is a trivial matter to blab to everyone about how they dream and hope to kill Americans and destroy the American military bases in their lands. They then become astonished at how the enemies of Allah ask him about these things when they interrogate him, and he wonders how they knew about it?!"*

Maqdisi also complains that many jihadist attacks are not carried out for strategic benefit but because such attacks are easy:

*"There are other young enthusiasts who oppose us by attacking churches or killing elderly tourists, or relief agency delegates—and other such trivial targets—whereby they do not consider what will benefit the da'wah [call to religion], jihad or Islam, nor do they give preference to what will cause most injury to the enemies of Allah. Rather, their choice is only based on the easiest target."*

Maqdisi describes the best mujahideen as those who are "*looking for targets that will bring down the enemy combatants and defy them—such as nuclear weapons, or intelligence centers and political posts, or centers of legislation and economy in the land of the polytheists*".

Maqdisi also criticizes those who attack Shiite Muslims, objecting to the attacks on both theological and practical grounds. In a 2005 interview with al-Jazeera, he said that ordinary Shiites could not be held responsible for their beliefs: "*The laypeople of the Shiite are like the laypeople of the Sunna, I don't say 100 percent, but some of these laypeople only know how to pray and fast and do not know the details of the [Shiite] sect*". This pragmatism does not contradict his intellectual hatred for Shiite teachings, saying in This Is Our Aqeedah: "*We declare our hostility toward the path of the Rawafid [the Shiites] who hate the companions of the prophet and curse them.*"

Maqdisi frequently writes that hating non-Muslims is an Islamic duty. In his 1984 book, The Religion of Abraham (Millat Ibrahim), he says that this hatred "*should be shown openly and declared from the outset.*" In *An Appraisal of the Fruits of Jihad*, he writes that any attacks on non-Muslims are theologically justified regardless of whether they result in any progress toward creating, or "consolidating," an Islamic state and regardless of changing political circumstances: "*Any fighting done for the sake of inflicting injury upon the enemies of Allah is a righteous, legislated act, even if it brings about nothing more than inflicting this injury, angering the enemy [and] causing them harm.*"

Simultaneously, however, he argues that for strategic reasons the mujahideen should at present concentrate their efforts on trying to establish a pure Islamic state in the Muslim world, saying that "*one of the greatest tragedies of the Muslims today is that they do not have an Islamic state that establishes their religion on the earth*." He also says that "*the mammoth, accurately planned operations that were carried out in Washington and New York, despite their size, they do not amount to more than fighting for injury*"—i.e. that they were justified only because they killed non-Muslims but had no strategic benefit. Importantly, however, he also says that if such attacks make it harder for the mujahideen to consolidate and build a true Islamic state, they should be avoided.

Through his writings which simultaneously justify both extreme violence and tactical pragmatism, Maqdisi has gained an iconic status in radical circles at a time when many jihadis—perhaps including even Osama bin Laden and Ayman al-Zawahiri—are becoming increasingly discredited. As a result, a public retraction of his more extreme views would send shockwaves through the jihadist community; on the other hand, a systematic recalibration of jihadist theory focusing attacks on Western military installations and secularists in the Arab world could reinvigorate the jihadi movement and perhaps win it new followers. Given that Jordan has reportedly forbidden Maqdisi from speaking publicly as part of the conditions of his release, it seems unlikely that his views have changed while in prison.

A poem allegedly written by Maqdisi in May 2007 tellingly describes a conversation between himself and the prison authorities in which they tell him: "*Renounce [your views]; many shaykhs have... Renounce and you will be generously rewarded with material [benefits]. In return, you shall [have freedom to] speak*". Maqdisi records his response as "*Prison is sweeter to me ... My suffering for the sake of religion is sweet.*"

If Maqdisi has indeed remained loyal to his ideals, much will depend on how much freedom Jordan's government gives him to propagate his ideas; Maqdisi has consistently shown himself willing to continue promoting jihadist ideology regardless of the personal consequences.

# Abu Basir & Abu Qatada

Abu Basir al-Tartusi is another prolific contemporary scholar of Syrian origin. He is a slightly more moderate Salafi ideologue who resides in London, more often criticizing past jihadi mistakes and urging caution and selective action. His tone is due in large part to the scrutiny he was put under following the 2005 London train bombings. He has provided scholarly arguments to back armed resistance to tyrannical rule (*by employing jihadi tactics*), also prefaced on the importance of Muslims living by the Sharia.

Abu Qatada al-Filistini, born in 1960 in the West Bank, is another example of a Palestinian-born cleric who encourages jihad against apostate rule in accordance with the Sharia and is among the most frequently cited authors in the study. His writings contend that, according to the Sharia, it is every Muslim's individual obligation to overthrow and expel any secular government from Muslim lands by bombing, sabotage, coup, or other means available to them that would advance the implementation of Sharia in that land.

These Salafi scholars play a critical but not widely observed role in the global jihadi movement. Ideology is often overlooked and is considered separate from the strategic and operational aspects of Islamist militancy. Yet, the scholars behind the jihadi movement set the framework for debates and provide direction that is by and large adhered to, or is at the least a determining factor in the planning of attacks. By better understanding their role in the movement, governments combating terrorism can attempt to intervene earlier in the radicalization process and ultimately work toward undermining their influence.

# The "salafi" conflict

After the war in Iraq started, Zarqawi quickly became one of the most wanted terrorists in the world. As the leader of al-Qa'ida in Iraq, he was involved in the killing of hundreds of Iraqi civilians and the beheading of US citizen Nick Berg before being killed by an American air strike in 2006. These actions were also noticed by other radical Islamists, including Zarqawi's former mentor, Abu Muhammad al-Maqdisi. In 2004 and 2005, the latter criticized Zarqawi for his extreme use of violence. This criticism and the conflict between them that followed are the subject of several academic publicationsas is the claim that al-Maqdisi's critique was a sign of revisionism. The same is true for the arguments between the supporters of the two men and how this conflict led to the establishment of a fatwa council to "protect" jihad from faulty practices.

The division among Salafi-Jihadis in Jordan started in mid-2005 when al-Maqdisi directed an open letter entitled "Munasara wa Munasaha" (Advocating and Advising) to the leader of al-Qaeda in Iraq, Abu Musab al-Zarqawi, criticizing him for targeting Shiite and Christian civilians and accusing al-Zarqawi's organization of being infiltrated by Jordanian security. The shaykh also emphasized the importance of mujahideen leadership being in Iraqi hands.

A few weeks later, al-Zarqawi responded to al-Maqdisi's letter, arguing that the latter's criticism did not have a negative impact on him but instead sabotaged the "jihad in Iraq." These accusations caused divisions to erupt between sympathizers of both parties, a situation intensified by the recent emergence of the so-called the "Neo-Zarqawists."

Similar posts have increased noticeably in jihadi forums, indicating that the division between the "neo-Zarqawists" and the "Maqdisists" is becoming deeper and suggesting that the radical faction of Salafi-Jihadis is growing in Zarqa. Although the mainstream Salafi-Jihadis (as represented by the Maqdisists) are fighting back, the neo-Zarqawists see themselves as inheriting the legacy of Abu Musab al-Zarqawi, which may play a major role in attracting young extremists to this new faction.

Several scholars briefly acknowledge that these discussions and the subsequent rifts between Jordanian radicals after 2004 are rooted in the 1990s, though there is a lack of literature on this period. It was in the 1990s that Zarqawi, Maqdisi, and several other like-minded Jordanians are said to have formed a group known as *Bay'at al-Imam*, or "Fealty to the Leader."

# Bay'at Al Imam

The group known as Bay'at al-Imam formed during a time of regional and national turmoil in Jordan. In the early 1990s, the Middle East witnessed the first Palestinian intifada, the American-led invasion of Iraq after the latter's occupation of Kuwait in the 1990/91 Gulf War, and renewed efforts to start an Arab-Israeli peace process in Madrid in December 1991. Meanwhile in Jordan, economic problems forced the regime to raise taxes and cut subsidies, which caused prices to rise and led to protests throughout the country.

These tensions were exacerbated by the arrival of several hundred thousand Palestinians with Jordanian citizenship who were expelled from Kuwait due to the Palestine Liberation Organization's support for the Iraqi regime during the Gulf War.

One of these Palestinian returnees was 'Isam al-Barqawi, who had adopted the name Abu Muhammad al-Maqdisi, and would eventually help found the radical Islamist group mentioned above.This turmoil caused great disillusionment among many Jordanians. Economic hardship, uncertainty about the large scale in migration of Palestinians, the ease with which the American-led coalition invaded Iraq with the help of several Arab regimes despite widespread popular opposition, and the start of a peace process with Israel caused some Jordanians to lose faith in their regime altogether.

As a result, some disillusioned men began to look for radical solutions to these problems. Consequently, a disparate number of Islamist groups with vague, but radical ideas emerged in the early 1990s and engaged in violent acts against Christians, liquor stores, nightclubs, and Jordanian officials.

This trend of radicalization was reinforced by the return of the so-called "Afghan Arabs," i.e., Arabs who had gone to Afghanistan to fight the Soviet occupation and the Afghan communist regime, but later returned to their home countries. These "Afghan Arabs" were not welcomed home by the Jordanian authorities upon their return and often ended up living in poverty, frustrated by their inability to find work. With the military experience they had gained in Afghanistan, these men made a crucial contribution to the violent groups that were set up in Jordan in the early 1990s.

One of these returning "Afghan Arabs" was Ahmad al-Khalayila, who would later be known as Abu Mus'ab al-Zarqawi. Zarqawi and Maqdisi, who had also spent time in Pakistan and Afghanistan but focused on teaching there, seem to have first met in the Pakistani city of Peshawar, in the home of fellow "Afghan Arab" Abu al-Walid al-Ansari.

It is not entirely clear what their relationship was like in Peshawar, but the two met again in Jordan after Zarqawi returned from Afghanistan and Maqdisi from Kuwait, where he had moved after leaving Peshawar. According to Maqdisi, Zarqawi was "yearning to help the unity of God and the call to God."

The two attracted a group of mostly poor, uneducated young men of both Palestinian-Jordanian and East Bank Jordanian origin, some of whom had fought in Afghanistan as well. These men seem to have followed Maqdisi because he had already written nu-merous books and articles, therefore offering precisely what they had lacked: a coherent ideology.

On the basis of al-Maqdisi's radical ideas of applying takfir (excommunication) to the regimes of the Muslim world because of their alleged unwillingness to apply shari'a in full, these men formed a group that later became known as Bay'at al-Imam. Although very little has been written about "Bay'at al-Imam," much of the existing literature that does pay attention to the group describes it in far more violent terms than is justified by the available evidence. Some simply refer to the group as a "terrorist organization."

Others label it one of many "radical jihadist groups . . . whose task was to ignite a revolutionary jihad" and that was willing to use "terrorist tactics or an "anti-monarchist jihadi underground."Some even go so far as to label it "a global Jihadist recruiting network," used by Maqdisi and Zarqawi to "coordinate the movement of Jordanian fighters in and out of Afghanistan," without offering any evidence for this argument. The members of "Bay'at al-Imam" were certainly radical, but the available evidence is far less conclusive than the idea of "Bay'at al-Imam" as a "jihadi"

The first reason "Bay'at al-Imam" cannot be described as a terrorist organization is that the group formed by Maqdisi and Zarqawi never used this name in identifying itself. Its members are said to have named their group only informally and to have referred to themselves mostly as Jama'at al-Tawhid (the Society of the Unity of God) or, especially, Jama'at al-Muwahhidin (the Society of the Upholders of the Unity of God).

As one of the group's leaders, Maqdisi was adamantly against the use of the name "Bay'at al-Imam," stating that it "is a fabricated name about us that the intelligence services have stuck on us"

The name "Bay'at al-Imam," which was later used by the Jordanian press and courts to describe the Jama'at al-Muwahiddin, was not entirely fabricated, but the name of a different group altogether. During the Gulf War, a Jordanian man called Nabil Abu Harithiyya (also known as Abu Mujahid) started a group called *Harakat Bay'at al-Imam* (the Movement of Fealty to the Leader) together with another Jordanian, Ghanim 'Abduh.

Abu Harithiyya is said to have been a friend and neighbor of Maqdisi's brother-in-law, and 'Abduh was a member of the Jordanian branch of Hizb ut-Tahrir, a radical but nonviolent pan-Islamic group with branches across the world. Together, Abu Harithiyya and 'Abduh issued several communiqués in the name of this group, which believed that the Jordanian regime was un-Islamic. 'Abduh allegedly wrote a treatise entitled *Ba'yat al-Imam* that argued for believers to pay allegiance to a religious leader, or *imam*

He showed the document to Maqdisi, who liked the idea in principle, but found it impractical. Because Abu Harithiyya was later arrested and sent to prison together with Maqdisi, Zarqawi, and other members of "Bay'at al-Imam" (i.e., Jama'at al-Muwahhidin), the intelligence services likely assumed that they all belonged to one and the same group called Bay'at al-Imam.

Given the plethora of radical groups in Jordan at the time, the lack of clarity around the name "Bay'at al-Imam," and the ideological closeness between the actual Bay'at al-Imam and Jama'at al-Muwahhidin, it is quite possible that the intelligence services themselves confused or con-flated the two groups, not being able to make heads or tails of all the different names. A second reason "Bay'at al-Imam" cannot be labeled a terrorist organization is that it was not an organization, in the sense of being a structured and organized group. In fact, "Bay'at al-Imam" seems to have been similar to the many other groups that came into existence in the early 1990s, in that it was quite informal and loosely organized.

Members of Bay'at al-Imam usually met in one another's houses,as some individual members, such as Sharif 'Abd al-Fattah (known as Abu Ashraf) and Abu al-Muntasir have confirmed. Meetings were also held in mosques in various towns throughout Jordan, such as the 'Abdullah bin 'Abbas Mosque in al-Zarqa'.

The group was so informally organized that Maqdisi did not even associate the name Jama'at al-Muwahhidin with the group's actual members in Jordan, but simply equated it with his personal religious advocacy in which he had been engaged for years, even before he came to Jordan.

A third reason to reject the labels "terrorist group" or "jihadi organization" for "Bay'at al-Imam" is that it suggests that the group was primarily or even entirely concerned with planning violent action against civilians or the Jordanian regime. While there are some indications to support this view, a closer look at the literature on the group reveals that the character of the group and the nature of its activities are not consistent or clear. Several authors mention some plans for violent attacks in which "Bay'at al-Imam" was supposedly involved, but none of the plans resulted in actual armed operations.

Moreover, their information is based on the confessions of Zarqawi and Khalid al-'Aruri, another member of "Bay'at al-Imam," to the Jordanian State Security Court (SSC) or appears to come from a former intelligence official.

Given the reputation of the Jordanian General Intelligence Department (GID) with regard to the use of torture of political prisoners to induce forced confessions that can subsequently be used in the SSC, this information is suspect. Furthermore, considering the large number of radical groups active in Jordan in the early 1990s, such plans may have been wrongly attributed to "Bay'at al-Imam."

Notwithstanding the above, "Bay'at al-Imam" was caught planning one armed attack. Many sources mention that Maqdisi, after returning from Kuwait, had brought some weapons with him that had been abandoned by the Iraqi army after it pulled out of the country, which Maqdisi himself confirmed.

In 1994, after an Israeli settler called Baruch Goldstein had murdered 29 Palestinians in the Ibrahimi Mosque in Hebron, some members of "Bay'at al-Imam" wanted to plan an attack on Israel to avenge them. It is said only two members were engaged in planning this attack, namely 'Abd al-Hadi Daghlas and Sulayman Damra (also known as Sulayman Hamza).

Maqdisi reluctantly issued a fatwa to permit this operation, stating that it was legitimate, but that he himself preferred to focus on spreading his message in Jordan.

However, the plans were discovered by the Jordanian security services before the attack took place, along with the weapons that Maqdisi had smuggled out of Kuwait. As a result, the whole group was arrested and tried as "Bay'at-Imam" in 1994.

In the end, 16 men were sentenced to 15 years imprisonment for involvement in this operation. "Bay'at al-Imam" was thus only involved in one attack that we can be certain of, and it is likely this was indeed the only one.

Moreover, this one attack never materialized due to intervention by the security services. If this "terrorist group" did not engage in terrorism, with what kind of activities did it keep itself busy? Their main activities were spreading their message through missionary outreach (da'wa), as well as organizing lessons and sermons that Maqdisi gave in people's houses throughout Jordan.

Members of "Bay'at al-Imam" also copied the writings of Maqdisi and distributed them among like-minded men. On called *Millat Ibrahim*(The Community of Abraham), which Maqdisi wrote in 1984. In this book, Maqdisi argues that contemporary Muslim rulers show loyalty to what he refers to as "man-made laws" (qawanin wad'iyya) instead of to the shari'a, which violates the unity of God (tawhid ), which should be present in all spheres of life, especially legislation. He calls on Muslims to disavow (bara'a) these regimes by declaring them apostates (murtaddun).

Another book by Maqdisi that builds on this idea is *Al-Dimuqratiyya Din* (Democracy Is a Religion), in which he writes that democracy, because it is based on the idea that the people and their laws are the ones who decide things — not God and the shari'a, is actually a different religion. Consequently, Maqdisi asserts that those who are aware of this idea and still consciously support democracy through voting and parliamentary politics are unbelievers (kuffar ).

Given the fact that the Jordanian regime had organized parliamentary elections in 1989 and 1993 — the first in decades — this was a highly topical issue, and Maqdisi's book on the subject played an important role in spreading his views among Jordanian Islamist radicals.

When the members of "Bay'at al-Imam" were put on trial, the group's message of rejecting "man-made laws" and regimes that made such laws spread to a wider audience. Members of the group consciously used the platform they were given to denounce the court, the judge, the "man-made laws" on which the justice system was based, democracy, and the Jordanian regime.

While "Bay'at al-Imam" may not have been the "jihadi" (i.e., using armed violence) or "terrorist" organization that it has been described as, the group was unapologetically radical. The way in which this radicalism should be expressed, however, was disputed among the group's members. Some, most prominently Maqdisi, argued in favor of *da'wa* (proselytizing), while others, including Daghlas, Damra, and possibly Zarqawi too at this point, favored a more violent approach. Moreover, they probably also disagreed over what target to attack: Israel or the Jordanian regime.

When the members of "Bay'at al-Imam" were imprisoned, they continued their *da'wa* activities as if nothing had changed. The aforementioned Abu al-Muntasir claims that he regularly preached on Fridays, and fellow "Bay'at al-Imam" member 'Abd al-Hadi Daghlas also gave numerous sermons in the mid-1990s that were later collected and printed.

While most of these missionary activities seem to have been directed towards the group's own members and the other prisoners, this was apparently not always the case. According to one source, for example, a prison warden once informed Zarqawi that the Jordanian interior minister was going to visit them and told him and another inmate to "try to have a nice chat (*kalaman hilwan*) with him to show that you have changed so that you can go home."

Zarqawi allegedly answered the warden, "We have come here to call to Islam (*li-nad'u li-hadha al-din*), not to go home." When a group of politicians eventually came, Zarqawi warned them "by God the Most High, to be in the ranks of Islam (*fi saff al-Islam*) and not to help anyone against your brothers, the upholders of the unity of God."

Being the scholar of the group, Maqdisi was greatly involved in these *da'wa* efforts, and went even further in his attempts to engage prison personnel. In several pieces he wrote in jail, for instance, Maqdisi describes how he tried to explain to guards why — despite their own protestations — they were not

Muslims, but actually unbelievers because they worked to protect and uphold an unIslamic regime and its laws.

Maqdisi appears to portray his own position in these conversations as that of a scholar with superior knowledge. This is not just apparent from the fact that the guard in one of these debates speaks Jordanian Colloquial Arabic while Maqdisi speaks Classical Arabic, but also from his use of *takfir* against a warden of one of the prison's departments. The warden and Maqdisi both apparently considered each other to be unbelievers, but Maqdisi claims that his excommunication of the warden carries more authority because it is based on "much Islamic legal evidence (*adilla shar'iyya kathira*) that I have shown you several times," while the warden's is not.

Such nonviolent, yet confrontational behavior is bound to elicit a response from others, which is precisely what happened. Bitter debates occurred between fellow Islamist prisoners from the radical, but doctrinally different Hizb ut-Tahrir that sometimes ended with the parties accusing each other of unbelief.

One non-Islamist prisoner recalled how he came to know "Bay'at al-Imam" in prison and was shocked by their ideas, believing they would tear society apart with their willingness to brand some people who disagreed with them as infidels, and even wrote an article to warn others about them.

Prison personnel were cautious, if not hostile towards the radical members of "Bay'at al-Imam," frequently moving them from one prison to another in order to keep members apart and stop them from recruiting new followers. There were regular conflicts between the group's members and the personnel over violence against inmates and the wearing of prison uniforms. Members of "Bay'at al-Islam" are said to have protested such measures with the limited means at their disposal, which included blocking doors or refusing to follow daily routines.

While "Bay'at al-Islam"'s activities in prison were largely nonviolent, members' recollections of a particular incident perhaps illustrate the group's motivation behind their missionary activities. This incident suggests that some members of "Bay'at al-Imam" thought that they were part of a divine plan to resist the "infidel" regime inside prison. In this conflict, prison guards hurled tear gas canisters at the prisoners, leading 'Abd al-Hadi Daghlas to shout, "We have come to die!" The prisoners reportedly noticed, however, "that God honored them so that the gas thrown at them by force did not affect them." When the inmates protesting their treatment later went to sleep, one of them had a dream about the Prophet Muhammad's army commander Khalid bin al-Walid and his companions coming to help the prisoners, telling the dreaming inmate not to worry because God would meet the requirements of the believers. When Zarqawi heard about this dream, he was delighted and considered it a sign.

Throughout its existence, "Bay'at al-Imam" had been an informally organized group, as shown above, and up until this point had not had a real leader. According to Abu al-Muntasir, however, Zarqawi and Khalid al-'Aruri argued from the time before their imprisonment that the group should have an official leader.

Abu al-Muntasir claims that they decided early on that Zarqawi would be the group's leader, while Maqdisi would be in charge of missionary activities, though it is unclear what this meant in practice. It seems obvious that a loosely organized group without a clear idea of what to do would naturally gravitate towards Maqdisi with regard to da'wa because of his seniority in knowledge and experience. When the group went to prison, its members organized, and Maqdisi is said to have then become its leader.

However, after prison guards beat a member of the group, leadership shifted from Maqdisi to Zarqawi, when the former was allegedly reluctant to take action after the incident. Although Maqdisi himself claims that he and the rest of the group successfully protested the supposed insults to Islam by the prison personnel, it is clear that the admiration he enjoyed from the group was mostly due to his knowledge, not his leadership skills. As a result, Zarqawi was made the new leader of "Bay'at al-Imam."

Maqdisi himself would later claim that he gave up leadership of the group willingly in order to focus on writing and teaching, but he would also down-play the matter by stressing he was only resigning the leadership of a small group, and not a state or anything important.

Maqdisi's account may be a correct description of what happened, due to his inclination towards da'wa. Nevertheless, it seems that the two men's reputations began to diverge from this point onward. In the few pages dedicated to "Bay'at al-Imam" in the existing secondary litera-ure, perhaps no other issue features as prominently as Zarqawi's personality. He is described in various publications as a tough man of action when he was in prison, who used makeshift weights to keep himself fit and was aggressive towards those who got in his way.

Given this toughness (ostensibly developed in Afghanistan and during his former career as a petty criminal) and loyalty to his fellow prisoners, Zarqawi seemed a natural leader in prison, where such characteristics are presumably seen as important qualities. This was also apparent in his treatment of other prisoners, whom he appears to have subjected to a strict regime, dictating what they should wear, what they should read, and when they could watch television.

Zarqawi's personality — characterized as it was by toughness, action, and discipline — contrasted sharply with that of Maqdisi. Not only was the latter a middle-class man of Palestinian origin — unlike the poor, East Bank Jordanian Zarqawi — but he was also friendly in his approach towards others, focused on reading and writing, and was perhaps more submissive in the face of violence.

Maqdisi is described as an easygoing man in prison who had normal relations with people, even those with whom he disagreed, and as someone who was very preoccupied "with knowledge", sometimes to the annoyance of others.

It is tempting to conclude from this that Maqdisi was a compromising and weak man, while Zarqawi was the exact opposite, as Abu Qudama Salih al-Hami — Zarqawi's brother-in-law and admiring biographer — has indeed concluded. Hami states that the other prisoners "considered [Maqdisi] to be opportunistic.

Although Hami's personal grudge against Maqdisi for criticizing Zarqawi means that his description of Zarqawi should be treated carefully, it seems that Maqdisi was indeed much friendlier and more tolerant than Zarqawi. Nevertheless, a Jordanian lawyer involved in the case of "Bay'at al-Imam" claims that members of the group were tortured by the General Intelligence Directorate, and several of their fellow prisoners claim that Maqdisi was one of them.

In fact, Hami himself writes that torture exacted a heavy toll from Maqdisi and that, apparently after one particularly brutal torture session, *"some of his brothers did not [even] recognize him until he recognized them himself . . . and they cried over his condition."*

This suggests that descriptions of Maqdisi as weak or feeble are exaggerated and that he probably could only be described as such in comparison with Zarqawi, who did seem to possess much more of the personal qualities a leader of radical Islamist inmates needs.

This became particularly clear when the members of "Bay'at al-Imam" were released as a result of the royal amnesty following King 'Abdullah II's succession to the throne in 1999. After his release, Maqdisi stayed in Jordan to continue his missionary activities, while Zarqawi, Daghlas, and several others went abroad to engage in jihad. Maqdisi has made it clear that their decision dismayed him, but also that he was not surprised, given Zarqawi's (and perhaps others') lack of patience to study and focus on da'wa

While the strict security situation in Jordan was a push factor in motivating members of "Bay'at al-Imam" to go abroad to relocate, the lure of al-Qa'ida's global jihad also acted as a pull factor for many radicals. This brings us to a final dimension of the differences between Maqdisi's and Zarqawi's leadership: jihadi authority.

While differences in personality and, to a lesser extent, ideological disagreements between Maqdisi and Zarqawi are mentioned in existing literature as a cause for their breakup, the issue of jihadi authority is entirely absent. Jihadi authority refers to the perceived status to speak authoritatively on armed jihad. One might expect Islamic scholars to have the most authority in this regard since they are experts on the religion from which jihad stems. This is true to a certain extent, and it is probably also the reason why some radical Jordanian Islamists flocked to Maqdisi in the early 1990s.

As time went by, however, it seems that the members of "Bay'at al-Imam," particularly when they were in prison, started favoring jihadi experience (i.e., having actually fought in a jihad) over religious knowledge on this subject, leading to a simultaneous devaluation of Maqdisi's status and a rise in Zarqawi's.

Though both Maqdisi and Zarqawi had gone to Afghanistan, only the latter had actually fought there, even if he came too late to fight the Soviets. The question of combat experience in a successful jihad against Afghanistan's Soviet occupiers and local communist regime became increasingly important to establishing jihadi authority among radical Islamists in general, and among members of "Bay'at al-Imam," in particular, during the group's imprisonment.

Romanticizing of the Afghan jihad was not uncommon and could also be seen in Zarqawi's behavior in prison. Several authors state that he is said to have worn Afghan clothes in prison and that he took credit for his participation in battles in Afghanistan, but they only mention this in passing.

It seems, however, that such things were part of a development in which participation in the armed jihad in Afghanistan came to be seen as a quality that trumped all others in establishing jihadi authority.One former fellow inmate who was imprisoned with "Bay'at al-Imam" speaks highly of Zarqawi and several other members of the group, precisely because they fought in an actual jihad, as opposed to Maqdisi, whom he despises for not having done so, but nevertheless had the temerity to criticize Zarqawi.

Another former fellow prisoner states that, once in prison, the "Afghan Arabs" were increasingly divided into two groups: one consisting of men who had actually fought in Afghanistan and another comprised of people who had merely been there, but had not participated in combat. The former, he states, were seen as heroes, while the latter often joined them in admiration.

This is confirmed by Hami, who writes that there were "Afghan Jordanians [in prison] of whom none had [actually] gone to Afghanistan". He also stresses that the group had three leaders in prison prior to Maqdisi, at least two of whom had extensive experience in the Afghan jihad. This contrasts sharply with Maqdisi, about whom Hami keeps reminding his readers that "he was not a known fighter (muqatil) or jihad fighter (mujahid) who lived between the bullets, the missiles, and the tanks for [even] a day".

Given his lack of fighting credentials in Afghanistan, Hami claims Maqdisi knows little about jihad and does not have the authority to rule on issues in this regard. Hami states that the mujahideen perceive a reality that Maqdisi and others like him do not understand.

The mujahideen, he states, acquire "knowledge of Islam through a way that is higher (asma), purer (asfa) and deeper (a'maq) than [that of] those who read and study it while they are behind their desks."

Considering such high regard for combat experience at the expense of scholarly knowledge, as well as the presence of several prisoners who had actually fought in Afghanistan, it is not surprising that having participated in the Afghan jihad became a mark of distinction for the members of "Bay'at al-Imam" and others.

# Back to the Future

Military action is necessary to halt the spread of the ISIS "cancer," said President Obama. In his much anticipated address, he called for expanded airstrikes across Iraq and Syria, and new measures to arm and train Iraqi and Kurdish ground forces.

Missing from the chorus of outrage, however, has been any acknowledgement of the integral role of covert US and British regional military intelligence strategy in empowering and even directly sponsoring the very same virulent Islamist militants in Iraq, Syria and beyond, that went on to break away from al-Qaeda and form 'ISIS', the Islamic State of Iraq and Syria, or now simply, the Islamic State (IS).

Since 2003, Anglo-American power has secretly and openly coordinated direct and indirect support for Islamist terrorist groups linked to al-Qaeda across the Middle East and North Africa. This ill-conceived patchwork geo-strategy is a legacy of the persistent influence of neoconservative ideology, motivated by longstanding but often contradictory ambitions to dominate regional oil resources, defend an expansionist Israel, and in pursuit of these, re-draw the map of the Middle East.

Now despite Pentagon denials that there will be boots on the ground – and Obama's insistence that this would not be another "Iraq war" – local Kurdish military and intelligence sources confirm that US and German special operations forces are already "on the ground" here. US airstrikes on ISIS positions and arms supplies to the Kurds have also been accompanied by British RAF reconnaissance flights over the region and UK weapons shipments to Kurdish peshmerga forces.

Early during the 2003 invasion and occupation of Iraq, the US covertly supplied arms to al-Qaeda affiliated insurgents even while ostensibly supporting an emerging Shi'a-dominated administration.

Pakistani defense sources interviewed by Asia Times in February 2005 confirmed that insurgents described as "former Ba'ath party" loyalists – who were being recruited and trained by "al-Qaeda in Iraq" under the leadership of the late Abu Musab Zarqawi – were being supplied Pakistan-manufactured weapons by the US. The arms shipments included rifles, rocket-propelled grenade launchers, ammunition, rockets and other light weaponry.

These arms *"could not be destined for the Iraqi security forces because US arms would be given to them"*, a source told Syed Saleem Shahzad – the Times' Pakistan bureau chief who, "known for his exposes of the Pakistani military" according to the New Yorker, was murdered in 2011. Rather, the US is playing a double-game to "head off" the threat of a "Shi'ite clergy-driven religious movement," said the Pakistani defense source. This was not the only way US strategy aided the rise of Zarqawi, a bin Laden mentee and brainchild of the extremist ideology that would later spawn 'ISIS.'

## Dividing Enemies

According to a little-known report *"Dividing Our Enemies"*, made by US Joint Special Operations University (JSOU), post-invasion Iraq was an interesting case study of fanning discontent among enemies, leading to 'red-against-red' [enemy-against-enemy] firefights. While counter-insurgency on the one hand requires US forces to ameliorate harsh or deprived living conditions of the indigenous populations to publicly win local hearts and minds.

In other words, US forces would pursue public legitimacy through conventional social welfare while simultaneously de-legitimizing local enemies by escalating intra-insurgent violence, knowing full-well that doing so will in turn escalate the number of innocent civilians *"caught in the crossfire."* The idea is that violence covertly calibrated by US special operations will not only weaken enemies through in-fighting but turn the population against them.

In this case, the 'enemy' consisted of jihadists, Ba'athists, and peaceful Sufis, who were in a majority but, like the militants, also opposed the US military presence and therefore needed to be influenced. The JSOU report referred to events in late 2004 in Fallujah where *"US psychological warfare (PSYOP) specialists"* undertook to *"set insurgents battling insurgents."*

This involved actually promoting Zarqawi's ideology, ironically, to defeat it: *"The PSYOP warriors crafted programs to exploit Zarqawi's murderous activities – and to disseminate them through meetings, radio and television broadcasts, handouts, newspaper stories, political cartoons, and posters – thereby diminishing his folk-hero image,"* and encouraging the different factions to pick each other off. *"By tapping into the Fallujans' revulsion and antagonism to the*

*Zarqawi jihadis the Joint PSYOP Task Force did its 'best to foster a rift between Sunni groups.'"*

Yet as noted by Dahr Jamail, one of the few unembedded investigative reporters in Iraq after the war, the proliferation of propaganda linking the acceleration of suicide bombings to the persona of Zarqawi was not matched by meaningful evidence. His own search to substantiate the myriad claims attributing the insurgency to Zarqawi beyond anonymous US intelligence sources encountered only an *"eerie blankness"*.

The US military operation in Fallujah, largely justified on the claim that Zarqawi's militant forces had occupied the city, used white phosphorous, cluster bombs, and indiscriminate air strikes to pulverize 36,000 of Fallujah's 50,000 homes, killing nearly a thousand civilians, terrorizing 300,000 inhabitants to flee, and culminating in a disproportionate increase in birth defects, cancer and infant mortality due to the devastating environmental consequences of the war.

To this day, Fallujah has suffered from being largely cut-off from wider Iraq, its infrastructure largely unworkable with water and sewage systems still in disrepair, and its citizens subject to sectarian discrimination and persecution by Iraqi government backed Shi'a militia and police. *"Thousands of bereaved and homeless Falluja families have a new reason to hate the US and its allies,"* observed The Guardian in 2005. Thus, did the US occupation plant the seeds from which Zarqawi's legacy would coalesce into the Frankenstein monster that calls itself "the Islamic State."

**Camp Bucca**

Beyond conspiracy theories – which are often justified in an era where everything appears as though it is part of a plan or a scheme – we have the right to ask why the majority of the leaders of the Islamic State (IS), formerly the Islamic State in Iraq and Syria (ISIS), had all been incarcerated in the same prison at Camp Bucca, which was run by the US occupation forces near Omm Qasr in southeastern Iraq.

In the context of conspiracy theories, there are a lot of rumors about links between IS and the US intelligence or affiliated organizations. But to what extent are these theories credible? Is there evidence that corroborate them?

These questions seem legitimate, provided that ready-made answers are not accepted without convincing evidence. However, it is difficult to get this kind of evidence, and we might need another Edward Snowden or WikiLeaks to learn the real truth about the relationship between IS and US intelligence.

Yet not having this evidence should not prevent us from trying to gather some clues that may not amount to definitive evidence, but which will no doubt question the narrative that fully exonerates US intelligence from involvement with the jihadis.

First of all, most IS leaders had passed through the former U.S. detention facility at Camp Bucca in Iraq. So who were the most prominent of these detainees?

Abu Ayman al-Iraqi... also "graduated" from Camp Bucca, and currently serves as a member on IS' military council. The leader of IS, Abu Bakr al-Baghdadi, tops the list. He was detained from 2004 until mid-2006. After he was released, he formed the Army of Sunnis, which later merged with the so-called Mujahideen Shura Council.

What happened during Baghdadi's detention in Bucca remains a mystery. Some press reports said he had been detained as a "civilian" in prison for 10 months in 2004, while other reports stated he was captured by the US forces in 2005 and held for four years at Camp Bucca. This latter possibility is unlikely, given that Baghdadi had formed the Army of Sunnis and joined the Mujahideen Shura Council shortly before the assassination of Abu Musab al-Zarqawi in June 2006. This is while bearing in mind that this council was established in January 2006, which makes it more likely that Baghdadi had been released either in late 2005 or early 2006.

It should be noted that after the Army of the Sunnis merged with the Mujahideen Shura Council, the Americans were able to successfully hunt down the leaders of al-Qaeda in Iraq, starting with Zarqawi in 2006, and not ending with Abu Omar al-Baghdadi and Abu Hamza al-Muhajir in 2010, the death of the former being the event that paved the way for Abu Bakr al-Baghdadi to become the organization's leader.

Another prominent IS leader today is Abu Ayman al-Iraqi, who was a former officer in the Iraqi army under Saddam Hussein. This man also "graduated" from Camp Bucca, and currently serves as a member on IS' military council.

Another member of the military council who was in Bucca is Adnan Ismail Najm. He was known a(Abu Abdul_Rahman al-Bilawi). IS named the operation for the "invasion of Mosul" after him. He was detained on January 2005 in Bucca, and was also a former officer in Saddam's army. He was the head of a shura council in IS, before he was killed by the Iraqi army near Mosul on June 4, 2014.

Camp Bucca was also home to Haji Samir, aka Haji Bakr, whose real name is Samir Abed Hamad al-Obeidi al-Dulaimi. He was a colonel in the army of the former Iraqi regime. He was detained in Bucca, and after his release, he joined al-Qaeda. He was the top man in ISIS in Syria, but was killed in Aleppo in the first week of January 2014.

According to the testimonies of US officers who worked in the prison, the administration of Camp Bucca had taken measures including the segregation of prisoners on the basis of their ideology. This, according to experts, made it possible to recruit people directly and indirectly. Former detainees had said in documented television interviews that Bucca, which was closed down in September 2009, was akin to an "al-Qaeda school» where senior extremist gave lessons on explosives and suicide attacks to younger prisoners. A former prisoner named Adel Jassem Mohammed said that one of the extremists remained in the prison for two weeks only, but even so was able to recruit 25 out of 34 inmates who were there. Mohammed also said that U.S. military officials did nothing to stop the extremists from mentoring the other detainees.

While Camp Bucca is the common denominator among most IS leaders, another one is the fact that a majority of them were officers in the Baathist army, which explains the ease with which the radical group has been able to infiltrate the clans and coax some of their leaders into joining its ranks.

Another noteworthy point is that none of the leaders who had emerged out of Bucca and who were subsequently killed, were killed in U.S. airstrikes, but rather at the hands of the Iraqi army, the Syrian army, or in fighting with other armed groups.

What had happened in Bucca then? What were the circumstances that made all those former detainees subsequent leaders in the extremist group? These questions require answers and serious investigations. No doubt, we will one day discover that many more leaders in the group had been detained in Bucca as well, which seems to have been more of a "terrorist academy" than a prison.